"*Discipleship with* determined to eq life. It provides ea economics into th invoke innovative ... meaningful and transformational."

Artie M. Lindsay, Teaching Pastor Tabernacle Community Church

"This book is highly accessible and practical. It provides both 'why' and 'how:' why church leaders need to make an emphasis on faith, work, and economics central to their discipling work for the sake of their marketplace and millennial congregants, and how actual congregations have learned this language, awakened to its vital place in the Grand Biblical Narrative, and implemented doable, replicable action steps to equip the flock in applying this teaching in their daily lives for their good and the common good."

Dr. Amy L. Sherman, author, *Kingdom Calling: Vocational Stewardship for the Common Good*

Discipleship with Monday in Mind

How Churches Across the Country Are Helping Their People Connect Faith and Work

by Skye Jethani and Luke Bobo

Discipleship with Monday in Mind: How Churches Across the Country Are Helping Their People Connect Faith and Work

---

Published by Made to Flourish
www.madetoflourish.org

Cover Design: Brannon McAllister
Interior Design: Carson Cheatham, The Useful Group

Published and printed in the United States of America

ISBN: 978-0-692-84621-6
Religion / Christian Life / Devotional

Contents

Preface

Made to Flourish is an organization dedicated to encouraging and equipping pastors and churches to better connect Sunday to Monday. We frequently refer to the pyramid (page 8) when communicating our vision for how faith, work, and economics (FWE) can be integrated into the local church. To fulfill our mission, we begin by teaching pastors on the vital importance of striving for personal wholeness and then we provide pastors with rich theological content that underscores the importance of teaching their congregants FWE theology at the foundational level.

Pastors are introducing this rich theology to their churches through four main channels: corporate worship, pastoral practice, discipleship, and mission. The top of the pyramid represents churches that have embraced these ideas and practices and are finding ways to reproduce both pastoral leaders and congregational leaders. As new pastors are formed with these values and practices, they may serve in other churches, or plant new ones with the same DNA.

This book grew out of conversations we've had with many pastors across the country who have intentionally committed to these ideas and seen them influence the practices of their local churches.

Envisioning FWE Integration In The Local Church

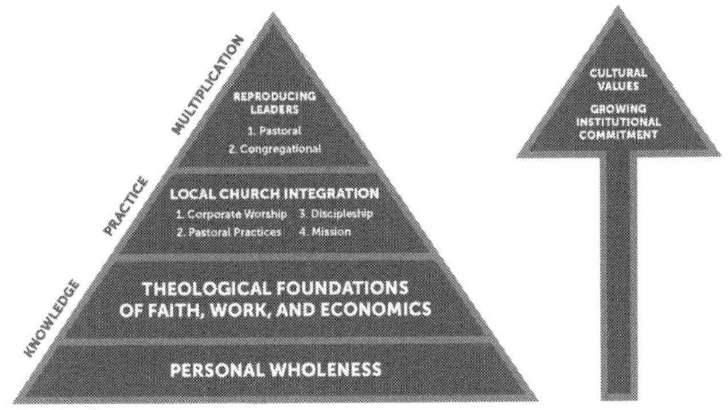

Foreword

I remember a wise mentor repeatedly reminding me of the need for leaders to have clarity of purpose and mission. One of his favorite phrases still rings in my ears. "If there is a mist in the pulpit, there will be a fog in the pew." Good advice for sure, but what happens when there is fog in the pulpit?

A few years into my pastoral ministry, I was forced to confront this compelling question. In spite of my pastoral diligence, packed schedule, and the best of intentions, there was a dense fog in my pulpit. I faced an inconvenient truth. I had been committing pastoral malpractice. I had spent the minority of my time equipping my congregation for what they had been called by God to do the majority of their lives. Rather than narrowing the Sunday to Monday gap that many in my congregation were experiencing, I had actually been helping it widen. My impoverished theological vision was impairing our congregation's spiritual formation, our contribution to the common good, and our local church's gospel mission.

Pastoral repentance was in order. I am most grateful for Christ Community Church, a gracious congregation that was ready to forgive my failings and move forward, guided by a more robust theology of vocation. In *Christian Mission in the Modern World,* John Stott concluded that, "We must begin with vocation." But what does this mean? I believe it means that we must see the entire biblical text as a coherent narrative of creation, fall, redemption, and consummation, revealing God's design and desire for human flourishing. I also believe we must regain the transforming truth that the gospel speaks to every aspect of human existence, calling us to discipleship in all areas of life.

Scripture tells us that, as image bearers, we have been created by a working God – with work in mind. That means, in part, that we have been created with community and collaboration in mind; work is not an isolated activity, but an interdependent one. We presently live in a broken and fallen world where our work is not what it ought to be. The good news is that, through the redemptive work of Jesus, the work we do and the workplaces we inhabit are profoundly changed by the gospel.

For those of us who have been called to the pastoral

vocation, the implications of a more robust theology of vocation and ...discipleship reshape not only our thinking, but also our pastoral priorities and practices. Our reading diet will adjust to help us better understand the Monday world of our congregation. A pastoral visit to the workplace of a congregation member will become as common as a visit to the hospital. Our preaching will look and sound differently. Our discipleship and spiritual formation pathways will change. With a growing understanding of the church's mission in the world, we will enthusiastically embrace our congregation's everyday work life. We will grasp with new conviction and passion that economic flourishing matters and that a primary work of the church is the church at work. Empowered and guided by the Holy Spirit, the local church we serve will be more faithful to Christ and more effective in furthering the common good.

This is why my heart leaps with joy that you are carving out time to read and reflect on what pastors across the country are doing to help their people connect Sunday to Monday.

I am most grateful for the many opportunities to roll up my sleeves and serve the Made to Flourish pastor's network. I pray that this book will inform your mind, strengthen your pastoral practice, enliven your worship experience, stir your heart, and ultimately shape the congregations and cities you serve. May our churches be all Jesus desires them to be, and may we who have been called to the pastoral vocation one day hear: "Well done good and faithful servant, enter into the joy of your Master."

Tom Nelson
Senior Pastor, Christ Community Church
Leawood, KS

Introduction

Three Pathways into the Faith, Work, & Economics Conversation

We live in an age of incredible innovation. Technologies change at breakneck speeds, and cultural trends appear and disappear just as quickly. Ministry is not immune from these forces. Anyone serving in church leadership in recent years has seen any number of ideas rise, peak, and recede again—each one claiming to be a movement of God and the answer to our challenges. As one pastor said, "I've tried every church renewal movement that has come down the pike—you name it, I've done it. I feel like a cork being tossed around on the sea."

We sympathize with this pastor's experience because it's been ours as well. When supposedly grassroots movements in the church turn out to be AstroTurf—artificially created by gifted marketers to sell products or fill conferences—it is easy to become disillusioned. How do we discern what is a genuine awakening of God's Spirit in the church and what is just another fleeting trend?

In recent years, there has been growing interest around the intersection of faith and vocation—what we prefer to call "Faith, Work, and Economics" (FWE). We have seen a significant increase in the number of books on the topic, as well as more conferences for both ministry and marketplace leaders. As we have traveled around the country engaging this topic, we've encountered skeptical pastors. "Is faith and work just the latest ministry trend?" they ask. Is it just the next wave that will toss them and their congregation in a new direction, leaving both more disillusioned when the ride is over? Is FWE something Christ is cultivating in His church that demands our attention, or is it merely more AstroTurf? This chapter will help answer that question.

We interviewed pastors from around the country who have been integrating faith, work, and economics into their ministries to learn how they were introduced to the topic. What led them to change the way their churches functioned, how they structured discipleship and outreach, even how they preached and allocated their time? By examining what paths led them to FWE integration, we wanted to discern whether it was addressing a genuine or manufactured need within the church.

After dozens of interviews, we found three recurring pathways. By looking at each one you may see similarities to your own journey. More importantly, you will begin to see how God may be using FWE to bring wholeness and integration to the church's mission in the world.

Pathway One: Through the Marketplace

Throughout my college and seminary years, I (Skye) had a variety of jobs to make ends meet, but I never really identified with any of those marketplace roles. Ministry was my calling. The other jobs were just vehicles for me to fulfill my ecclesiastical goal. After a decade in church leadership, however, my vocation changed. For the first time I found myself outside a pastoral position.

Suddenly everything was different. I was in the marketplace more than the church, and in the pew more than the pulpit. The adjustment was not easy. The most unsettling part was how the shift challenged many of my assumptions about ministry. With a 50-hours per week job, a young family, and precious little free time, I simply could not engage in many of the church's programs and activities—the same programs and activities I advocated as vital for spiritual growth when I was a pastor. I also began to hear sermons differently. It occurred to me that sermons rarely, if ever, addressed what

I did Monday through Friday. Of course, I had ignored non-ministry vocations during my decade in the pulpit as well.

It was only when I left my pastoral role that my blind spots were revealed, and seeing ministry from the point of view of the marketplace is what led me to explore the biblical connection between faith and work. Looking back, I wonder how long my blind spots would have persisted had I not left my church leadership position for a season.

My introduction to FWE is not unique. A significant number of pastors we interviewed identified experiences in the marketplace as what awakened them to the importance of this topic. Some, like me, became curious about faith and work during seasons away from ministry, but most shared significant marketplace experiences that shaped their faith before entering ministry.

Jon Tyson, pastor of Trinity Grace Church in New York City, is one example. Tyson came to faith in Christ as a young man while working as a butcher's apprentice in Australia. The hours were long and the physical labor was intense. "I was wrestling deeply in my soul," he recalled. "What on earth does the gospel have to do with cutting up meat? I mean, what difference does it make?"

Being zealous for his new faith, Tyson wanted to leave the butcher's shop to serve God in ministry, but his legal apprenticeship bound him to the butcher for another four years. "I wondered how God could redeem that time," he said, "and I began to think about what it means to do everything to the glory of God." At first Tyson believed this meant using his time in the butcher's shop for evangelism. "I tried to evangelize the guts out of the place." (That's interesting wording for a butcher.)

As his faith matured, Tyson came to see butchery itself as a way to glorify God. "I would go to the shop before everybody else, get down on my knees, and hold my knife up as an offering to God. Then I would make each slice of meat an act of worship. I became really good and won Apprentice of the Year."

Tyson admitted that had he moved immediately into pastoral ministry, he probably would not have wrestled with questions about faith and work. His experience in the butcher's shop made him more sympathetic to the members of his own church called to vocations other than church work. His own search for a faith that integrated his life with God and his life at work has profoundly influenced how Tyson has structured the congregations he now leads.

When we asked Tyson to share a story of a church member who has adopted this theology of faith and work integration, he recounted the story of Lindsey, a former neighbor. Lindsey is a schoolteacher in the Bronx, and she absolutely loves kids. Our church

was making these vocational vignettes; stories about people in all kind of industries. These weren't stories about how much people loved their small group or how much they liked singing on the worship team. They were stories about people in their jobs. Lindsey got a vision for
this and I started to challenge her to think through questions about her field, education. What is the redemptive vision for education? There are so many factors—dealing with core curriculum, navigating a school system's bureaucracy, competitiveness among teaches, etc. Then she began asking questions of her own 'What do you do with negligent parents? What about kids from underprivileged homes, kids who come from homes with no food?' As she wrestled with these questions, she began to develop her theology of education. She saw that there was often little a teacher could do directly. There were systemic issues that needed to be addressed. So she went back and got her masters degree in education to establish credibility. After graduating, she became an educational consultant to principals. Now she can affect the whole system by influencing the leaders of entire schools. In this new role, she also influences teachers in training, shaping the way they will teach. Her ultimate goal is to work with the Board of Education. She hopes to help reshape its policies in a way that improves the entire educational system. But it all started with a few important questions.

Many other pastors shared similar stories about their

pre-church work. One was a basketball scout in Europe. "I asked myself a lot of questions," he said, "like why does the game of basketball even matter?" Another was a hairdresser. Like Tyson in the butcher shop, at first he saw the salon as a venue for evangelism. Later, he began asking deeper questions about how the gospel might apply to all areas of life—even cutting hair.

These experiences in the marketplace generated questions and confusion that prompted further investigation and study. Rather than viewing their early marketplace experiences as a wilderness period before starting public ministries, these pastors have come to recognize how the Lord was actually preparing them for ministry while they were serving in the marketplace. They were coming to see the feeble forms of faith that have dominated much of the church. They were learning how to sympathize with future church members called to invest most of their time outside the church. And they were identifying theological questions about mission and meaning that would eventually transform the way they preach and minister.

Pathway Two: Through the Millennials

While time spent in a vocation outside the institutional church has proven to be valuable for some pastors, not all of them came to the conversation about faith, work, and economics through that pathway. Many others discovered a need to integrate faith and work because of challenges they faced within the church, particularly while ministering to young adults—the generation known as the millennials.

Millennials, perhaps more than previous generations, are confronting many of our assumptions about both our theological categories and our philosophies of ministry. This book cannot examine all of the research about young adults nor is that our purpose, but a few characteristics of the generation did factor heavily in the interviews we conducted with pastors and may explain why the issue of work is felt more acutely by members of this generation in the church.

First, millennials are delaying marriage much longer than their parents or grandparents did. That may not seem like a significant fact, but most of us have inherited or created church structures that assume adults are part of nuclear families. As a result, our ministries and discipleship often focus on household relationships. Two decades ago it would have been very unusual for a 30-year-old in the church not to be married. Now it is often the opposite—it is odd if they are married. Fewer millennials are asking questions like, "How do I love my spouse?" or, "How can I raise my children in the faith?" Instead, more are asking questions like, "What does my work have to do with God's mission?"

Second, millennials carry a strong sense of calling and

interest in activism. It has become a stereotype today that all young adults want to "change the world" because of an inflated sense of self-esteem, but this generalization may have some basis in reality. Lawrence Ward told us that the millennials he ministers to don't like talking about "careers" as much as "callings." They want to believe their work is more than a job for personal advancement. They want to understand how their work relates to a larger vision; how it contributes to the common good and even to God's cosmic purposes.

Research from a number of organizations shows that millennials are not attending churches at the same rates as earlier generations. This fact has some church leaders scrambling to find strategies for reaching young adults. As Ward reported, "When I started talking about faith and work and economics, I started to attract Millennials." Surveys from the Barna Group confirm his experience. Barna found young adults who remain engaged with a local church are four times more likely than those who drop out of church involvement to say, "My church teaches me how the Bible relates to my career."

Unfortunately, most pastors have not wrestled either theologically or practically with matters of faith, work, and economics. They aren't equipped to address the questions central to the lives and identities of most millennials. Jon Tyson discovered this when he began a young adult ministry in Orlando. "We had a ton of college students coming and many who were moving into their careers. They were telling me, 'I'm on fire for God, but what do I do with the rest of my life?' I had a strong realization that my theology was inadequate. I couldn't answer them."

John Crawford, a pastoral intern at Redemption Church, and millennial himself, says the lack of answers is why so many of his peers are giving up on the church. He told us:

"All the studies show that one of the primary reasons my generation is leaving the church is because they don't understand how their Sunday experience of faith connects to their daily life from Monday to Saturday. There's a disconnect between their faith and their work. A lot of churches aren't engaging that discussion. They don't have a big theology or understand the fullness of the gospel. I think that's contributing to millennials' disillusionment with Christianity."

Imagine someone coming to your church asking how Christian faith could help their struggling marriage. Most congregations would have a buffet of resources from classes and Bible studies to pastoral counseling and archived sermon series. It is almost inconceivable that a church wouldn't be able to help that person. Why? Because we have embraced the household and family as an essential venue of discipleship. But for millennials, especially unmarried millennials, who are seeking to integrate faith and work—most churches are woefully unprepared.

Discovering this inadequacy, either through ministry with millennials or some other group within the church, is the second pathway leading church leaders into the faith, work, and economics conversation.

Pathway Three: Through the Scriptures

We pastors are bookish people. We have our noses in our Bibles a lot, and if they're not in a Bible they're probably in some other theological tome. Therefore, it should not surprise you to learn that nearly every pastor we interviewed credited Scripture—and often some historical theologian's explanation of Scripture—for their introduction to faith, work, and economics.

This third pathway was so important that it's helpful to see the first two pathways outlined in this chapter as tributaries flowing into it. Experiences in the marketplace and challenges ministering to millennials often made pastors aware of their deficient theology of work or disintegrated philosophies of ministry, but these questions then drove them back to the Scriptures to find answers.

Many of us assume that if we've attended seminary we were given a comprehensive theological training or enough training to meet the practical demands of pastoral ministry. However, very few of the pastors we spoke with said their introduction to faith, work, and economics came during their academic training. Ryan Beattie, a pastor at Bellevue Presbyterian Church, captured a common experience:

"It's amazing that I made it all the way through a Master of Divinity degree and years of fulltime pastoral ministry with such a weak faith-and-work theology. It's all over the Bible, from Genesis to Revelation. It's amazing to me that in all of my studies no one challenged me to think more about it."

In most cases, the challenge to think more deeply about faith and work came to pastors long after seminary and from two main sources. The first was Scripture itself. Jim Mullins explained how he ministered with a "truncated understanding of the biblical story." Practically speaking, his Bible "began in Genesis 3 and ended at Romans." He confessed, "It didn't include creation and new creation."

Mullins is not alone. A number of pastors we interviewed said that a deeper study of the opening and concluding chapters of the Bible transformed their understanding of both our work and God's mission. Many had seen work as a negative consequence of the Fall (Genesis 3), but a closer examination of Genesis 1 and 2 uncovered God's original intent for humanity and our work in his world. Like marriage, work was inaugurated before sin entered creation; it was part of God's good design for humanity and must be included in our redemption.

Similarly, we found that a deeper examination of

eschatology, the study of last things, also challenged many pastors to rethink the dualism that was inherent to many of their ministries. They were functioning under the assumption that much of the present created order, including work, carried no eternal value and that only church-related vocations had heavenly significance. Simply put, their view of the future led them to ignore work. It belonged to the "earthly" category while church-related work was deemed "spiritual." A closer reading of the New Testament, however, shattered these categories and led pastors to see God's intent to redeem "all things" through Christ.

The second source that challenged pastors beyond Scripture itself was historical theology. A number of church leaders we interviewed cited the writings of influential theologians of the past as playing a critical role in opening their eyes to the importance of faith, work, and economics. They realized this conversation was not new, and certainly not a recent trend fabricated by marketers or ministry conference organizers. It's been a vital element of Christian theology for centuries that has only recently been marginalized by some contemporary streams of the church.

Tom Nelson, for example, pastors Christ Community Church in Kansas City. His "epiphany" about the importance of faith and work came from his study of the Protestant Reformers. Names like John Calvin, Martin Luther, and

Abraham Kuyper were mentioned frequently by our group of pastors. It is important to note that not everyone came from Reformed backgrounds. Other pastors drew from their own Pentecostal theologies or social justice traditions to find historic roots for addressing faith and work.

Every pastor mentioned influential books from contemporary writers as well. In most cases these books helped the pastors piece together the parts of Scripture they had previously ignored or misunderstood, and introduced them to historic theologies of faith, work, and economics. (See a list of the most cited books in Appendix B.)

Modern ministry is bombarded with new trends. Discerning the significant from the fleeting is not easy. But we have found pastors with a lasting commitment to faith, work, and economics that have arrived at this conclusion through a combination of experience and theology. They have discovered the importance of an integrated approach because of their own time in the marketplace, or because they have found existing ministry priorities ineffective with young adults. They have also poured over Scripture and rediscovered long forgotten truths about God and humanity that have led to lasting changes in their approach to ministry.

Book Layout

We do not expound on this faith, work and economics

(FWE) theology in the proceeding chapters. Rather, the reader will find practical ways churches across the country have integrated this FWE theology into the life of the church. And scattered throughout this book are testimonials of Christians that are actually integrating this FWE theology into their Monday-to-Friday work.

Chapter 1
Pastoral Practice

Something remarkable happened to ministry in the middle of the twentieth century—it moved inside. Perhaps that is overstating the change. Pastors have served within churches as long as Christians have had purpose built facilities. What's changed is how much time most pastors spend within those buildings.

Consider what a typical church's ministry looked like a hundred years ago. Each Sunday the community gathered for worship, sacrament, and the preaching of Scripture, and the pastor often organized and led these Sunday gatherings. Like the rest of the congregation, however, the pastor spent most of his time Monday through Saturday outside the church building. He visited his church members in their homes, farms, and factories where he blessed their work and encouraged them to live faithfully with God and one another.

He also made calls to the sick and perhaps to those in jail. For most of Christian history ministry happened primarily outside the walls of the church, which is why most church facilities could remain relatively small.

Today, few pastors are trained to carry out their calling in this manner. Instead they are expected to stay inside the church all week, and their activities are usually focused more on operating programs and overseeing a staff than on the daily shepherding of the flock. When the sheep do require pastoral care, counseling, prayer, or instruction, only in rare circumstances—like hospitalization—is the pastor expected to leave his church office. Rather than engaging people where they work, we now expect the people to visit the pastor where he works. That represents a dramatic shift in pastoral practice from the previous nineteen centuries of Christian ministry.

The point of this history lesson is not to criticize newer modes of ministry or to awaken nostalgia for the past. Each has their strengths and shortcomings. Instead, we need to recognize how modern pastoral practices may help or hinder the integration of faith, work, and economics within our congregations today. As we interviewed pastors around the country with a commitment to FWE, we found that many engaged in practices uncommon among those trained in contemporary models of ministry. Instead, they were recovering pastoral habits from the past.

In this chapter, we will look at three of the most frequently cited pastoral practices. None of these are difficult to engage, nor do they require elaborate restructuring of a church's programming. These are activities an individual pastor or church leader may begin independently—no new programs to create or budgets to approve. For that reason, these practices may be the best place for a pastor seeking to integrate faith, work, and economics into their congregation to begin.

Pastoral Practice One: Curiosity

The first practice is more accurately identified as a proclivity. It's an attitude or disposition that the other practices are predicated upon. Although rarely identified as a pastoral characteristic, curiosity is an essential quality of any person called to shepherd and equip God's people.

One of the most frequent metaphors for leadership in Scripture is shepherding. David identified the Lord as his shepherd in the Old Testament, and Jesus referred to himself as the Good Shepherd in the New Testament. That is why throughout the Bible the leaders of God's people are also identified as "shepherds" (see Jeremiah 23 and 1 Peter 5). They are called to represent the character of God to his people. Even the title pastor means "shepherd."

What makes this metaphor so compelling is the trust and

intimacy that must exist between a shepherd and his sheep. The shepherd leads, feeds, and protects the flock. As Jesus said, "The sheep follow him, for they know his voice … I am the good shepherd. I know my own and my own know me" (John 10:4, 14). It is a profoundly relational image of pastoral leadership.

To shepherd well, a pastor must know his sheep. This was a trait we observed consistently among the church leaders we interviewed. They were incredibly curious about the people God had entrusted to their care. These pastors studied their congregations, they sought to understand their lives and contexts, and they gave particular attention to the vocations of their people. They wanted to know what their sheep did Monday through Saturday and how they did it. They were inquisitive leaders.

For example, when Jon Tyson first arrived in New York City to plant a church, he recognized that he could not effectively pastor his growing congregation without investigating their vocations. "I started subscribing to a bunch of emails about current events in various industries that particularly affected the people in my congregation," he reported. He still dedicates time every week to reading books about these industries. His goal is not to become an expert, but to be familiar enough to have meaningful conversations with people about their work.

Tyson says his commitment to studying the vocations of his church members and neighbors is often met with surprise. "I'll meet someone in a coffee shop or one of my neighbors and ask them what they do. When I share something I know about their work they'll say, 'Oh my gosh, you're a pastor? I can't believe you know about that.' It happens all the time."

Tyson is clear, however: "The goal is not to impress them but to connect with them." His curiosity continues to drive the conversation. "I tell the person that I actually don't know that much about their work," he said, "And I ask them, 'Please tell me more.' That puts me in the posture of being the learner and the other person in the position of the expert."

Like Tyson, other pastors reported that reading broadly in the industries represented in their congregations was very important, as well as not limiting one's studying to ministry principles or church management. "The problem with so many ministry books," one pastor told me, "is that they assume every church's context is the same. They offer plug-and-play solutions that may work in one place but not in another."

I (Skye) discovered this reality in 2008 not long after the full effects of the Great Recession were being felt. I was asked to speak at a church and consult with its leadership team. They were interested in learning how to attract more young adults to their church. After a few days, however, I discovered through thoughtful conversations with church members that a significant number of them worked in construction and real estate—two industries that were disproportionately impacted by the recession. I also learned that the CEO of one of the largest employers connected to the church had just committed suicide.

These facts drastically changed how I coached the church's pastoral team. "Your congregation is hurting right now," I told them. "They're scared about their jobs and worried about the future. This isn't the time to launch a new program to reach young adults." Although they had the best of intentions, the pastors' focus on reaching young adults had come from attending ministry conferences and reading popular ministry books. Put bluntly, they were more curious about what was happening in other large churches than what was happening in their immediate community. They didn't know their sheep.

Don't assume that practicing curiosity means immediately reallocating hours of your time to reading about agriculture or financial derivatives. It can be as simple as asking good questions. Kent Duncan, for example, says that when he meets with members of his church, he is much more intentional about asking about their vocation. It isn't a perfunctory question like, "How's work?" Instead, Duncan inquires more meaningfully. "Can you tell me about your work?" is a better question. He wants to understand the significance of what they do throughout the week.

This essential quality of pastoral curiosity grows when we begin to put the life and context of our sheep ahead of our agenda as shepherds–when we recognize that genuinely seeking to understand their callings is part of our calling.

Pastoral Practice Two: Workplace Visitations

Once a shepherd begins to cultivate a growing curiosity about the lives of the sheep, it will inevitably lead him or her out into the pastures where the sheep spend the majority of their time. In other words, curiosity pushes pastors outside the church walls and into the work environments of church members. Regularly visiting people at their work was by far the most cited, and most transformative, pastoral practice we uncovered in our interviews.

Most people are surprised when a pastor asks to visit their work. Pastor Mike Reading said he's been talking about faith and work from the pulpit for some time, but members of his church were still unsure what to think about his interest in seeing where they work. "I find that they're mostly like, 'All right, but what are you going to do if you come to my office?' They're concerned about how I will carry myself, but for the most part they are really flattered."

Reading says workplace visitations are essential for him to understand people's lives. "I go to where people work, eat lunch with them, try to see their office, try to know what they experience, because it fascinates me." These visitations function as reconnaissance missions for pastors like Reading. They provide a fuller picture of what the congregation's needs and opportunities really are. This information is valuable when planning sermons or church initiatives.

It also provides deeper insight into people's gifts and abilities. Reading shared about one church member he described as a "stoic intellectual."

> "This guy didn't show much emotion at all in church, but when I went to his office, he was like a kid. I never got to see that part of him before, but it came out when he worked."

Mike said that workplace visitation provided more connection points between what this church member was really passionate about and how he could actually have a place in the church.

Mike sees the time he spends in church members' offices as ultimately "fruitful and helpful to the church," but it also makes members "feel more affirmed and supported by the church." In other words, workplace visitation is a practice that simultaneously informs the pastor as it affirms the member.

Stan Archie likes to take things a step beyond mere visitations. He asks church members if he can do "ride alongs" where he'll spend half a day shadowing them at their work. Archie reported:

> "We had a guy who was a homebuilder at our church. I used to go to the sites with him and do the inspections together. That gave me a real feel for what his life was like, and it allowed me to make sure the church was offering legitimate, practical, biblical foundations for the reality of his daily living."

Some pastors might be uncomfortable asking a church member for a ride along, but starting to practice workplace visitations doesn't have to be difficult. Once again, it all starts with curiosity. Kent Duncan had a conversation with a church member who managed a printing operation. After a few questions about his work, Duncan learned they just purchased a new printing machine. "I'd like to come see that," he told the member. Now he's making plans to visit his congregant's workplace and start connecting with him there.

Obviously, some workplaces are easier to visit than others. Duncan reported, "With some blue-collar workers you can't always see them on the plant floor, but they're absolutely happy to talk about their work." When a pastor shows that he cares for them, prays about their work, and makes an effort to affirm it, "It is a very positive experience."

Other pastors shared creative ways to get outside the church building and into the workplace environments of their people. Meetings, as we all know, are a necessary part of every ministry. Larry Ward tries whenever possible to hold a meeting at the member's place of business rather than at the church. "I say, 'Do you mind if I come to your office?' That way I don't simply allow them to come to the church."

Jim Mullins and John Crawford have even taken many pastors' most isolating task, sermon prep, and moved it outside the church. Mullins reports:

> "A lot of our pastors prepare their sermons in the places where people live and move and have their being. Last week I prepared my sermon in a hospital cafeteria. Sometimes we'll go to industrial areas or onto the campus of Arizona State University. We want the places where our people live and work to shape the sermons we preach to them."

The interviews we conducted taught us that church leaders need to seek opportunities to get outside the church and into the workplaces of their people. Conduct one-on-one meetings, or even church committee meetings, in someone else's workplace. Meet church members at their office for lunch. Inquire about their jobs and ask to learn more by visiting the site. You may even find people willing to let you shadow them for part of the day. The information you gather and the affirmation you show is likely to transform both you and your church.

Pastoral Practice Three: Prayer & Counseling

Having a fuller understanding of church members' vocation and workplaces also shifts the way pastors pray for their people. This becomes visible in the worship gatherings (a topic we cover later in this book), but also in the weekly practices of the pastor between Sundays.

After Larry Ward started incorporating workplace visitations into his pastoral routine, he found more members were inviting him to their offices. A schoolteacher came to Ward and said, "Pastor, would you come to my classroom and pray?" The public school, for obvious reasons, wouldn't allow prayer in the classroom with the students, but Ward came in just before the students and prayed with the teacher, "and the school allowed us to do it." His presence and prayer helped the teacher see her work and classroom as a sacred calling and space. It shifted her vision of her work.

Another member of Ward's church oversees a laboratory that conducts tests on cells. He invited Ward to the lab to "pray over us as we do our testing." By getting out of the church and into the laboratory, Ward is affirming the value of these scientists' work and asking for the Lord's presence to empower their research.

Jon Tyson said that when he visits a workplace, he often asks the church member how they hope to see God's kingdom in their work. That often leads to prayer not just for the church member, but for the business and everyone who works there. Tyson told us of one ministry opportunity that has resulted from this practice:

> "We had a guy at our church with some influence within a startup business. It has now done really well. Sometimes he will reserve a conference room when I meet him there. The two of us will spend an hour praying together for the kingdom of God to come into that company, for the encouragement of its leaders, and for people's salvation."

To those who pass by it may look like Tyson is being interviewed for a job, but it's actually ministry that's happening.

Prayer is a significant way pastors care for their people, and so is counseling. Some of the church leaders we interviewed reported a shift in their counseling practices as well. "I view vocational counseling as just as important as marriage counseling," said Jim Mullins. "Both marriage and work are found in Genesis 1 and 2, but the church only tends to put effort into helping marriages. I think that is really important, but so is our work in the world."

Of course, in some cases being curious about church members' work may uncover serious problems requiring pastoral intervention. Jon Tyson, for example, said it is common in a place like Manhattan to discover a church member has made an idol of their work. Mike Reading shared the story of visiting a church member at his office and discovering his work was all-consuming. Reading recalled,

> "It prompted a great conversation about his tendency to give his best energy to his work and have nothing left for his family. Now I'm focusing on how to help his marriage. I don't think he would have been that vulnerable with me if he hadn't first felt affirmed by me in his work."

We have found that pastors who effectively integrate faith, work, and economics into their congregations engage in practices that take them outside the church and into the workplaces of their people. This changes how they pray, how they counsel, and even how they preach. It all begins, however, with curiosity—a genuine desire to understand the people entrusted to their care and the work God has called them to. The weekly routines of ministry change when shepherds make it a priority to know their sheep.

Chapter 2
Corporate Worship

Infusing New Language

The language we use when we gather as a church community is not neutral. If we're not careful our language can inadvertently perpetuate the unbiblical idea that spiritual work is superior to secular work. Language used in worship can also unintentionally elevate white-collar work while denigrating blue-collar work.

Artie Lindsay, pastor of Tabernacle Community Church, knows this tendency well and takes pains to avoid it. "We are very careful with our language," he says. Lindsay and others are careful not to use "secular/sacred" kind of talk or "full--time ministry" language. And all members at Tabernacle are constantly reminded, "You're valued and loved by God." They attempt to help all their congregants to see that *everyone* is in fulltime ministry. Of course, this emphasis dovetails well with biblical teaching of the priesthood of all believers (1 Peter 2:4-10).

When we asked Lindsay to share a story of a church member who has imbibed this theology of faith and work integration, he recounted the story of Vickie.

One of Lindsay's congregants, Vickie, has taken his teaching on the importance of faith-and-work integration to heart and it has influenced her work. Initially, however, Vickie, a Christian, was not even a believer in this faith-and-work integration idea. In fact, she was quite cynical that God cared about her work of making sure emergency room visitor's medical insurance was in order. When Lindsay began talking to Vickie about her work, Vickie was less than receptive. "Pastor Artie keeps talking about this, but doesn't know what I do. I am a paper pusher." However, as she continued to meet with Lindsay and listen to him, her heart softened. Eventually, she became a believer. Today she sees what she does in light of her faith. "God was using me to bring care to people during one of their most difficult and stressful of situations."

Pastor Tom Nelson adds:

"We have deliberately abandoned language that perpetuates the dualism of the world to elevate the spiritual world over the material world; we have jettisoned language that devalues the temporal in light of the eternal; we have 'retired' language that elevates certain vocations over others and language that diminishes the fullness of God's redemptive program and the goodness of all creation."

Nelson and his staff avoid phrases such as, "secular work," "kingdom work," "fulltime Christian work," and "moving from success to significance." They're similarly careful to avoid language that minimizes temporality. They avoid ideas encapsulated in expressions like "living for the *line* (eternity) rather than the *dot* (temporality)." They also try to eschew devaluing the material world with phrases like, "It is all going to burn," or "What really matters are people's souls." Another common phrase they've jettisoned is, "Make your life count for God," since it can diminish people's sense of their intrinsic value as embodied image bearers in the here and now.

Pastor Ryan Beattie intentionally invites worshipers to dwell on what happened during the week. Rather than asking they "forget about their cares and concentrate on God" in the corporate worship setting, Beattie asks, "Hey, what's on your calendar this week? We're going to sing songs that ask God for wisdom and courage and help [for your work week]. Don't leave [your work concerns] at the door." Beattie stresses the importance of infusing the church context with language around faith and work and the value of work before launching too many programs.

Some churches have gone a step further by incorporating faith and work language into their self-descriptions. At Abundant Life Church, Pastor Ward mentioned that they are governed by the motto: "a church where faith and life connects." Such language enforces the belief that faith should inform *all* of life, of which work is a significant part. Reading's church, United Evangelical Free Church in Seattle, Washington, has a motto for his church that is similarly wholistic: "Quit trying to be the best church in the city that competes with other churches, and be the best church *for the city*. Seek to be the kind of church that, if we were to shut our doors, the city would mourn."

At Jonah's Call[1], Jay Slocum and his pastoral staff have adapted a famous quote from the Dutch theologian Abraham Kuyper and made it their motto: "There's not a square inch that doesn't belong to Jesus." In fact, faith, work, and economics (FWE) is written into their church business plan! This has spilled over into the adoption of new language elsewhere in the life of the church. For instance, the director of music isn't called the "worship leader." Why not? Jay explains:

> "We don't want our people to think that worship is something that takes place merely on Sunday. It's something we do when we gather, and it's something we do when we scatter." In other words, work is a form of worship that, when done well and ethically, is done "heartily, as for the Lord" (Colossians 3:23-25).

[1] The theology of faith and work was a part of the DNA of Jonah's Call from the beginning.

The language pastors use can perpetuate the secular-spiritual dualism leading to a bifurcated life for congregants. Or a pastor's language can affirm all vocations as good and noble and promote the idea that our work provides a laboratory for growing into Christlikeness. As one pastor put it, "Our pastoral language must stimulate and support whole-life discipleship." [2]

Affirming All Vocations

All work matters to God. Collecting trash matters to God. Preparing lattes matters to God. Changing dirty diapers matters to God. Cooking a meal matters to God. Developing an Excel spreadsheet matters to God. As someone once said, "If it is not sinful work, it is sacred work." Work is not only sacred but an opportunity to worship. Freddy Williams and David Comstock eloquently explain, "The ability to work is a gift and a sacred practice. Work is an opportunity to worship, as we join God in the everyday invitation to represent Him."[3]

To communicate the sacredness of work, many churches have "Faith at Work" interviews during the worship service. For example, every six weeks, Pastor Brad Beier at Living Hope Church, interviews a church member.

---

[2] Nathan Miller Tweet, July 20, 2016.

[3] Freddy Williams and David Comstock, *Story Catechism*, p. 51.

During the interview, Beier asks five basic questions of the interviewee:

1. What type of work do you do?
2. How do you try to do that work as a Christian?
3. How does sin seem to affect that work?
4. How do you try to serve your neighbors through your work?
5. How can we pray for you?

Not only does Beier conduct "Faith at Work" interviews, he has also incorporated a version of this in their children's ministry. They take what they do upfront for the congregation and "reduce it into a more bite-sized package" for children. Child-friendly props are brought in, and teachers ask questions such as, "What do you want to do when you grow up?" and "How can you serve Jesus through that type of work?" The aim is to get children thinking about faith and work at an early age.

Pastor Mike Reading takes a different approach. They emphasize, celebrate, and affirm a different industry each month. In January 2016, it was education. In February it was finance. And recently it was celebrating those in the technology industry. Reading chooses a person in that industry to interview and he asks these basic questions:

1. What type of work do you do?
2. How did you feel called to do what you're doing?
3. What are certain opportunities or obstacles you're facing in your work?
4. How does your faith speak to those obstacles?
5. How can we pray for you?

At the conclusion of the interview, Reading invites all congregants in that particular industry to stand and he leads a commissioning service much like they would to commission a missionary going abroad.

Many churches do variations of what Reading and Beier do. For instance, Artie Lindsay conducts "all of life" interviews once a month. They have interviewed healthcare professionals, business owners, stay-at-home moms, and a student. After the interview, church leaders invite all people in that particular field to stand and the congregation prays for them together.

City Hope Church Pastor Jeremy Lile, who refers to himself a "recovering dualist," dubs these interviews as "stories of servants and stewards," based on 1 Corinthians 4:1 (NRSV). His questions are:

1. How do you cocreate with God through the work that you do?
2. Where do you experience the Fall and brokenness?

3. Where do you experience restoration and redemption through the work you do?
4. How do you sense that your work is part of God's greater work?

Thus far, Lile has interviewed a homeschool mom, who was involved in a ministry in their community to prostitutes, and an auto mechanic, who is one of the best mechanics in their region.

Pastor Jim Mullins, who has been doing such interviews over the past two years, believes that there is a positive cumulative effect. In particular, he has noticed that:

1. People have a sense of how God made them, and therefore of the good works that they are created to walk in.
2. People, in their work context, understand the stewardship mandate of Genesis 1 and 2 and what they are stewarding and what aspects of God's character are being reflected.
3. People have taken the command to "love your neighbor as yourself" seriously. And they see their work as a way of loving their neighbor.
4. People realize that the workplace can be a rich context in which to proclaim the gospel.

One unexpected result has been that local businesses have approached Mullins and his pastoral staff at Redemption

Church wanting to hire people from their church. And this includes businesses owned and operated by nonbelievers! One restaurant in particular, which is known as one of the nicest restaurants in Tempe, Arizona, has even asked Redemption Church staff to lead a retreat for their staff.

Commissioning Services

It is a common practice for churches to commission Christians who embark on doing missionary work abroad. Many churches see their congregants entering the workplace—a mission field—on a weekly basis. So, bi-monthly, Pastor Jason Harris at Central Presbyterian Church, commissions people to specific vocations in the same way they would pray for pastors or foreign missionaries. They have commissioned those in finance, law, the arts, and the health industry, so far. Harris explains that failure to do this "deepens the divide between the sacred and the secular."

Initially, people were not sure why Harris was praying for lawyers! Attorneys sometimes feel like second-class citizens in a church context because "lawyers" often received rough treatment at the hands of Jesus in the New Testament. When Harris told a few of the lawyers that he would be praying for them during the service, some were concerned that they would have to bear the brunt of a bad lawyer joke. However, it proved to be a moving and very ennobling experience for both the congregation and the lawyers to see them lift up the important work that lawyers do. By commissioning lawyers, Harris and others affirmed that these dear brothers and sisters took their vocation as advocates for their clients seriously.

Similarly, Ryan Beattie has planned and participated in four commissionings for those in many industries. Beattie, whose church is located in the shadow of Microsoft and Amazon, has commissioned workers in such industries as technology and computer and software engineering. He has also commissioned his congregants who labor in the fields of marketing, medicine, and finance.

Beattie explained that when they first began, they had to coax people to stand up, and they had to explain to the congregation *what* they were doing and why they were doing it. After commissioning those in the tech industry one Sunday morning, a female visitor hurriedly approached Beattie and said, "It's our first Sunday visiting here. My husband had never seen his faith relating to his work." The commissioning service was powerful for this man. Such examples simply underscore the fact that we were never meant to live a compartmentalized life; our faith should inform our parenting, our citizenship, and our work.

Pastor Jon Tyson who bumped into Steve Garber in Washington, D.C., recounted a conversation they had. Garber told

Tyson that he had heard about his work in New York and kindly offered him this suggestion:

> "There are people who labor all week long and you bring missionaries up front and you pray for them, and you commission and send them out. Wouldn't it be an amazing thing if you could take the people and send them into the city that you love so much, so that they felt like missionaries to their industries?"

Tyson recalled that the conversation with Garber had a "liturgical shaping force." Since that crucial conversation with Garber, Tyson has employed a new practice before preaching. Before opening the Word, he invites a person representing a particular vocation to come forward. For example, he might have a schoolteacher come up and read a prayer for all educators. Then all teachers are invited to stand and the congregation claps and cheers for them! And then they are commissioned to go and educate.

Such commissioning services can have a similar "liturgical shaping" impact on others. For example, after doing a commissioning service, a teacher approached Tyson and said, "That was the most powerful moment in *my entire life* in church. Thank you." Commissioning services have a powerful ability to affirm people in their work.

Traditional and Nontraditional Sermons

The sermon in a worship service provides an ideal time to teach on the importance of faith and work integration. Pastor Larry Ward, Abundant Life Church, does a sermon series around the Labor Day Weekend with a prayer and commissioning service. One surprising benefit of such preaching and teaching is that Abundant Life Church is attracting and retaining millennials.

As mentioned above, Ward told us that the millennials he ministers to don't like talking about "careers" as much as "callings." They want to believe their work is more than a job for personal advancement. They want to understand how their work relates to a larger vision—how it contributes to the common good and even to God's cosmic purposes. So, teaching on faith and work is helping their millennials to make a concrete connection on how they can use their knowledge, gifts, and talents to make a difference in the lives of others.

Sometimes in place of traditional sermons, Ward hosts "forums." These forums feature people from different occupations who talk about what they do and why it's beneficial for people. So far, Ward has had a funeral director, an insurance agent, and a human resources person participate in these forums. After presenting, the congregants are allowed to ask questions of the presenters. Often there are more questions than there is time to answer them. Ward doesn't mind substituting a forum for a traditional sermon because he wants his people to view work as part of the "all of life" discipleship process.

Pastor Kent Duncan, who did his doctoral work on introducing the theology and practice of faith, work, and economics to his mostly blue-collar congregation, developed a four-week, all-church study where each Sunday was devoted to a faith-work topic. Duncan noted that his context is particularly difficult because there is often animosity between upper management and those on the assembly line. Animosity is often exacerbated when management exhibits an attitude that says, "You do the work, we'll do the thinking. And by the way, we need more production out of you." That communicates to a blue-collar worker that their work does not matter. At the end of his sermon series, Duncan did a commissioning service for these blue-collar workers. These workers were brought to the front of the sanctuary and his elders came and laid hands on them. Then the entire congregation prayed that God would make these brothers and sisters flourish in their callings.

At the end of the prayer, one female member said, "That was the most significant prayer anybody ever prayed for me." Duncan found that his congregation was "wonderfully receptive to the whole series on work because he was finally talking about something that mattered to them." Work matters to God—and it matters to congregants, too.

Because the preaching moment is such an excellent opportunity to teach, Jason Harris tries to incorporate anecdotes and illustrations that draw from the variety of vocations represented by his members. Doing so, he said, speaks of those vocations in a way that affirms the dignity of the vocation. "There's a lot of people who may be in a particular profession, and when they hear the profession mentioned in the sermon, it's done in a very derogatory way." But by using stories drawn from the workplace that cast congregants' professions in a positive light, Harris is able to counter those negative perceptions and affirm their callings.

Chapter 3

Discipleship & Spiritual Formation

In Lester DeKoster's book *Work: The Meaning of Your Life* he explains that "half of our work is forming the world, and the other half of your work is the work forming you." On one hand, our work provides a laboratory for growing in Christlikeness. And on the other hand, we are forming the world through the agency of our work. In light of this dual purpose, we must integrate our faith and our work through intentional discipleship. Churches are seeking this intentional discipleship in diverse ways.

The Basics, Book Discussions & FLOW

In their discipleship setting, Reading starts with the basics.

> "I spend a lot of time connecting people to God's intent for creation, God's desire for industries, and the renewal of all things. The ships of Tarshish, the indus-

> tries—they're still going to be in the New Heavens and New Earth. The culture of cities and nations will still be there. It will be purified in glorifying God. I sense the biggest need is for my people to have a positive view of our city and culture. And it's been a very slow process to communicate that, especially with a city like Seattle, that can be so anti-Christian."

Pastor Jeremy Lile is currently going through a book with a group of men. In these groups, a space has been created where all are invited to talk openly about their successes and struggles that they are facing at work. Lile has also taken his larger community through the *FLOW*[4] series. He was delighted that this series led to robust conversations about God, work, and vocation. Likewise, Pastor Beier has hosted "Table Talk Discussions," an onsite Bible study for after Sunday worship. On a quarterly basis, Beier takes four to six weeks to focus on a discipleship topic with a group over lunch.

---

[4] *FLOW*, produced by Acton University, stands *For the Life of the World*. This accessible 7 episode video/digital series uses the prophet Jeremiah's letter to the exiles in Jeremiah 29 as a launching pad to instruct us what it means to live as "exiles" in our contemporary context. Perhaps the most insightful episode is the one on "Creative Service'"(episode #3). Here the *FLOW* creators demonstrate beautifully how our work, a creative service and an economic activity, contributes to a "mysterious, enormous, and organic collaboration with others or for the sake of the life of the world."

Beier also used *FLOW*—with some adaptation—because in his urban context many come from severely broken homes and many of the *FLOW* episodes present an idyllic picture of the family.

Pastor Artie Lindsay creatively convened what Tabernacle Community Church calls *LIVE* Team (Leadership in Vocational Engagement). Here, a group of 12 people read and worked through Amy Sherman's book, *Kingdom Calling*. The hope is to infuse these concepts into the life of the church. Another goal of starting with this twelve is so this core group develops a robust view of the kingdom, not only to impact the local congregation, but ultimately to impact the city as well. Tabernacle does not have an adult Sunday School. However, Lindsay wants to develop a faith, work, and economics curriculum for middle school students as a Beta test group to introduce them to a theology of work.

In-House Curriculum Development

Christ Community Church, under the leadership of Pastor Tom Nelson, has developed its own curriculum designed to provide guidance from "cradle to grave." The church's children's ministry has icons and banners prominently displayed with these words: *Ought* (Creation), *Is* (Fall), Can (Redemption), and *Will* (Restoration/Consummation). Nelson explains that the four-chapter story is embedded into the discipleship DNA of Christ Community Church.

Mullins and other staff at Redemption Church have also created their own curriculum in-house. However, Mullins admits that this development generally involves synthesizing a number of off-the-shelf materials.

Pastor Duncan's teaching and preaching was reinforced through concurrent small group Bible studies that explored his sermon topics more deeply. One topic they explored that is often overlooked in the FWE conversation is the significance of the Sabbath. Duncan's teaching sessions communicated the significance of this study to his members. The small group Bible study material was developed using materials such as "Work is Worship"[5] and adapted Acton Institute materials on economic and human flourishing.

When Duncan was asked for an example of a church member who has imbibed this theology of faith and work integration and is now living it out, he proudly spoke of Mike.

As you may remember, Duncan ministers to a congregation comprised mostly of blue-collar workers.

---

[5]"Work as Worship" is part of a DVD series with Matt Chandler, Norm Miller, and J.R. Vassar. It was produced by RightNow Ministries and is available online at RightNowMedia.org.

The importance of faith and work integration has been a hard sell for his congregation. However, Duncan relayed the story of Mike, a young man who worked at a local print shop cutting dog food labels. After listening to Duncan's sermon series on faith and work, and after going through the small group Bible study, Mike was able to make a connection between Adam's creative activity in the Garden in cooperation with God and his job of cutting dog food labels. He proudly said, "Even if I'm cutting dog food labels, I'm making something that wasn't there before. I'm cooperating with God in the creation of something new." This sharp young man is in Bible school right now training for ministry. But he appreciated the connection between his ordinary labor and what God wanted through his work at that time in his life.

Seminars

Instead of a traditional adult Sunday School, Central Presbyterian Church hosts a seminar series called *Vocare*. Pastor Harris described the purpose of this seminar format: "To explore the intersection between the gospel culture and vocation, thinking through how we live out our call as God's people in the world in light of the challenges and opportunities of our cultural moment." Speakers have included those from academia (like David Miller Director of the Princeton University Faith & Work Initiative and Steve Garber, principal of The Washington Institute for Faith, Vocation & Culture) and recently, practitioners who work in those particular vocations.

When Harris was asked to share the story of a church member who has imbibed this theology of faith and work integration and is now living it out, he recounted the following story about a CEO from his congregation.

Prior to moving to New York and attending our church, this CEO was living in another city, functioning as the head of a different company. They had purchased another company, and the acquisition required an enormous amount of time and energy on his part. It was a great success, and he was excited about being part of this accomplishment. But he told me that that following Sunday, as he sat in church, he had this sad moment where he realized that nothing that was happening at church spoke to what he'd been working on. No one knew. And even if they did know, it wouldn't have really mattered to them. I think for him this experience of sadness arose out of how deep this divide can be between the church and the workplace. So he, on more than one occasion, has told me just how much he has personally enjoyed and benefited from this seminar series. He has great thoughts on work and faith, and he feels like the seminar has been a massive encouragement to a lot of people in the church.

Shaping Children, Youth, and Families

Mullins admitted that there was a season where Redemption was focusing on people whose jobs already had honor and prestige in society (e.g., doctors, lawyers). They were also focusing exclusively on adults. So they started something called the "All of Life" camp. The name of the camp is drawn from the tagline of their church, "All of life is all for Jesus." The church takes children who attend the camp to various workplaces where adults are working, and they talk about their work. The goal is to give these students a rich experience within that particular work context. To reinforce what children are hearing on a typical Sunday morning and during the All of Life camps, parents are provided with materials so that they can discuss and reinforce the teachings with their children in the home (see Deuteronomy 6:4-9).

Vocational Affinity Groups

Some churches have started vocational affinity groups. The idea is to place Christians who serve in the same industry in a small group for mutual encouragement and instruction. Sustaining such groups can be challenging, but under the right conditions, these groups can be quite helpful.

Through their "Vocation Collectives," Mullins attempts to bring people from the same industry together one or two times a year. Here Mullins and other Redemption Church staff help these small groups facilitate a theological reflection on their work. These groups are also encouraged to meet and to pray for each other through the issues that come up in their work. For Redemption, the key to the sustainability of their vocational affinity groups is their infrequency. Group members are busy, which makes meeting weekly or even monthly unrealistic. But occasional "Vocation Collectives" meetings still foster relational connections that can be sustained outside of official meetings. These deep relational connections outlive the actual small groups. Nelson says that such vocational affinity groups have a relatively short shelf life unless "the relationships deepen into long-term valuable friendships."

Both Nelson and Mullins agree that sustained personal relationships should be the goal rather than sustained vocational groups. Jay Slocum has found that encouraging people to meet up during the natural rhythm of their workday—for example, at lunchtime or in the early morning before the workday begins—aids sustainability. Slocum explains:

> "We've empowered them to do really well in their vocations. They're working 50 or 60 hours a week and they're really 'killing it' in the marketplace. [As a consequence] they don't have a huge amount of bandwidth to be a good father or husband if they're taking one night during the week to do something away from their families."

When asked to share a story of a church member who has imbibed this theology of faith and work integration and lived it out, Mullins recounted the story of Mike and Jennifer.

Mike and Jennifer were passionate about work and their faith, but didn't know how to combine the two. "You have your spiritual life and you have your occupational life and hobbies you enjoy," Mike and Jennifer said. "We didn't see how the two connected," they added. They felt guilty, wondering if they enjoyed their occupations and hobbies too much. But when Mike and Jennifer caught a vision of how occupational endeavors—in their case, careers in the meat business—could fit into God's economy, and how they can serve and love their neighbors through them, they were enlivened. Eventually their newfound theology of work and faith drove them into getting the training required to become ranchers. It was a three-year process of learning how to run a ranch in a sustainable way that makes the best, healthiest meat. But they now run a ranch, and they have a theology of ranching!

Eight years ago, Tyson launched industry roundtables, which were organized around vocations. These "missional communities" went "very, very well," Tyson reported and they resonated with people in the community. These were midsize communities, organized around a particular industry. The purpose of the groups was to explore "theology, ethics, best practices, tensions, and networking." Tyson found that these groups fueled an appetite for further engagement. "Faith and work is like an itch that, once you start scratching it, you cannot stop scratching it." Unfortunately, these missional communities are no longer active. Though members of the groups were highly engaged, pastors are busy, and often simply do not have the time to facilitate getting folks beyond the surface to a deeper level.

Harris has started putting people together who are in the same industry—and just stepping back to see what happens. Recently, a group of CEOs of smaller companies gathered to learn from each other. Harris said the CEOs were grateful to connect with others who understood their challenges. "It's stressful being an entrepreneur and there are not a lot of people these CEOs can talk to about the kind of questions or problems they face."

Intensive Discipleship Schools

Some churches have opted to send their members to formal discipleship schools like Gotham Fellows School, Cascade Fellows,[6] and Surge.[7]

---

[6] For more about Cascade Fellows, see http://cascadefellows.com.

[7] For more about Surge, see http://surgenetwork.com.

When we asked Kim to share a story of a church member who has imbibed this theology of faith and work integration and lived it out, he recounted the story of a woman who started her own design studio downtown.

She became a Christian later in life, then came to Redeemer and went through the Gotham program. She saw her faith as being about serving to meet needs. In her case, that meant doing pro bono design work for nonprofits. What she didn't grasp was the way the gospel transforms everything she did in her workplace, not just how she could serve people in need. She began to look within her own organization to see what practices she and other senior staff were doing with their employees that really acknowledged their humanity and looked to develop them as human beings. She began to explore how she could give employees opportunities for creative expression. She also began examining the work she did, the clients that she would take. She was beginning and willing to take some pretty unorthodox kinds of clients because she wanted to be missional, and that meant going to areas that a lot of Christians wouldn't want to go. There was one client in Colorado who sold marijuana chocolate. She came to me, and we had a long discussion about whether this was something she should take on or not. I gave her enough theological background to wrestle through the question. For instance, in Scripture, God calls his people to be light in some pretty dark places. I wondered aloud whether God might be calling her into this area so that, through her relationships and the way she approaches her work, she might be a loving influence there. Ironically, as a result of going through a church program, she was more open to these clients than if she hadn't gone through it.

Pastor Beattie is a big fan (and alumnus) of the Cascade Fellows Program. Launched by Fuller Theological Seminary, Cascade Fellows is a rigorous nine-month program for Christian professionals who long for a deeper connection between their faith and their daily work. This intensive discipleship program, which offers two learning communities for both young and senior-level professionals, serves Christian professionals in a wide variety of callings including medicine, art, technology, business, engineering, education, and more.

At the time of this interview, Bellevue Presbyterian Church had two cohorts in the Cascade Fellows Program. These cohorts include students from other area churches as well. This program includes three retreats throughout the year. During six months, when there's not a retreat, the two cohorts gather for learning on Saturdays. These cohorts answer felt needs such as dissatisfaction with work. Beattie is finding that "applying the story of Genesis to the workplace of people who are committed to partner with God in their work, is empowering for the fellows." They have also put on two conferences: a Faith and Technology Conference and a Worship & the Arts Conference.

Pastor Mullins is an enthusiastic advocate of Surge. Surge is a twelve-month discipleship school that begins with a retelling of the four chapters of gospel story: creation, fall, redemption, and restoration. It is during the retelling of the whole gospel story that the instructors also address other topics such as idolatry and sanctification. After laying this theological foundation, the program emphasizes holistic mission. The last session focuses on work and vocation. Just from the Tempe, Arizona area alone, 250 people have matriculated through this intensive discipleship program. Mullins beamed as he recalled the program's impact. "The cumulative effect of having a new class go through it year after year and interact with each other is that this is really shaping culture."

When we asked Beattie to tell us a story of a church member impacted by the theology of faith and work integration, he told us about Julie.

Julie is a Cascade Fellow from last year who actually now is coleading with Beattie this year. She's a doctor in a physical therapy office and was ready to quit her practice. At one point, Julie was contemplating going back to school, doing something different; she didn't feel like there was a lot of room for her to develop and grow as a leader there. She felt burned out and frustrated in her job. After going through the Cascade Fellows Program, her perspective on work was transformed. Now she sees how her work matters. Julie often talks about the importance of the "little things." For example, when she begins working with a patient, the first thing she does when she puts her hand on a patient is to offer a silent prayer. She believes her work starts when she lays hands on a person, remembering that they are made in the image of God. Now her work is a holy thing to her. Julie realizes that her work is about bringing healing to her patients. Her new outlook has also had an impact on her career. A year and a half later, she's the Number Two person in her clinic! The program so transformed her perspective on work that she decided to stay. She felt called to this work and empowered to change it for the better.

Chapter 4

Mission & Outreach

At Made to Flourish, we speak about faith, work, and economics (FWE). Outreach and missions provide many opportunities to address the "E" in that acronym. We define economics as "the moral and social system of value exchange." Many churches interviewed have ventured into this area to help "the other." However, the approaches to missions and outreach vary widely in terms of how they play out.

Jay Slocum of Jonah's Call has a unique approach to outreach and missions. Jonah's Call does not have an outreach and missions budget per se. When people ask Slocum, "Why don't you give more to outreach?" he responds, "We give all of our budget to outreach." What does he mean by this? If their people aren't making the city flourish through their work, then they're failing. Slocum explains:

> "We may not be getting a lot of credit because we run a food bank, but we have people positioned in their careers as architects or teachers or lawyers or legislators or stay-at-home moms who are doing important work."

Slocum is trying to get parishioners to realize that, in the words of Lester DeKoster, "Half of our work is you forming the world, and the other half of our work is the work forming you."[8] In other words, our work does double duty. It forms us into being more Christ-like and we form our world through the agency of our work. It is the latter that Slocum is equipping his congregants to do.

Like-Minded Partners

Jeremy Lile is pastor of City Hope Church, a new start up church. In order to maximize their resources, they have pursued partners who are committed to like-minded efforts, like dignity-affirming work. Drawing from the ideas of John Perkins of CCDA[9] that "dignity isn't something that you give someone or take away from them," one of the couples at City Hope described a passion to "feed the hungry and to make

---

[8] From *Work: The Meaning of Your Life* by Lester DeKoster.

[9] The Christian Community Development Association (CCDA) and was started by John Perkins.

food security a reality in the city." All of this led to the starting of "an open-choice food pantry." As the description implies, people have choice in groceries that they select at the food pantry.

It's almost like assisted grocery shopping. Plus, the shoppers and those who help them share a meal together! This table meal creates a sense of community, and people now show up and say, "I don't even want groceries this week; I just want to be together as a community." This has taken time because most helpers only see their role as benefactors; people who give things away. Now they are seeing the usefulness of sitting at a table with people and getting to know their story and relating to them.

Lile spoke affectionately of a regular shopper who had been looking for work. When Lile saw him, he asked him how his job search was going. The man replied:

> "I just got a temp job, but I think it could develop into something long-term. Man, thank you guys so much. If it weren't for this place I probably would have lost my apartment because all my money would have gone to food instead of rent. It's helped me get by for these past five months as I've been searching for work."

Lile continued to tell us about the profound impact the shopping program has had on people's lives.

> "I've heard a lot of similar stories of people just saying thanks. It's not the typical image a lot of us have of people on welfare. It's often people who have just fallen on hard times because of the economic downturn and they needed that little extra boost. What I love to see is sometimes the people that are in line serving and hosting the guests jump out of line because their number gets called and now they're going through the line because they need a little help, too."

When we asked Lile to tell us about a church member who has imbibed and lived out faith and work theology, he told us about Brandon, an auto mechanic.

Brandon is the one of the top mechanics in Akron, Ohio. Brandon experiences the creativity of God in working on vehicles, seeing how intricate they are and how wonderfully they're made. And he senses the brokenness of the world because he's constantly working on broken things! Yet–Brandon is painfully aware that, as a bluecollar worker, he doesn't always get the respect extended to people in white-collar professions. And Brandon knows that people only come to him when there's a problem. Yet I've seen Brandon really affirmed in his position. Brandon was promoted to the role of shop foreman and has had opportunities to change the culture of his workplace. Formerly employees walked around the garage with their heads down. Now people walk with their heads high, a transformation achieved in part by affirming the work that they do. As Brandon felt his work affirmed, he, in turn, affirmed the work of others.

Newer churches like City Hope Church are not the only ones seeking partners to do outreach and missions. More established churches like Christ Community Church also see the value of partnering with like-minded friends. To that end, Christ Community Church has teamed up with Christ Fellowship Baptist Church, a church located in the urban core of Kansas City, Missouri. Nelson says that faith, work, and economics theology played a pivotal role in the partnership from the beginning. This is wise because for many churches located in the urban core, economic justice and equality is a central concern. Outreach and missions for Christ Community Church has involved hosting a conference with the theme of pursuing "Common Good" for the wider Kansas City metropolitan area. Speakers such as Greg Forster, Director of the Oikonomia Network at the Center for Transformational Churches at Trinity International University, and Brian Fikkert, founder and President of the Chalmers Center at Covenant College, have been invited to speak on the topic of faith, work, and economics. Fikkert shared a new vision for alleviating poverty at the 2015 Common Good Conference.

When we asked Nelson to share a story of someone deeply impacted by the theology of faith and work, he recounted the story of a business leader.

This business owner was designing his corporate headquarters. During the design phase he and his leaders started to think through not only how to treat their employees, but also the very spaces in which they would work. In particular, he thought through how his faith would shape the workplace itself and its design. He's deeply invested in a seamless faith, in his family. He wants to create a virtuous company with fair and equal policies and practices. But he's asking, 'How does my faith speak into my corporate headquarters in terms of the architectural space, structure, and how it's designed?' He's allowing the gospel to speak into every aspect of his life, personal and professional.

Nonprofits Make it Less Complicated

Many pastors found that the most effective way to promote faith and work integration was by starting a nonprofit. For example, in Woodlawn, located on the Southside of Chicago, Pastor Brad Beier told us that the unemployment rate is about 23%. So, as Beier led an effort to restore an old dilapidated building—formerly an old pool hall for hustling, prostitution, and drugs (that would later serve as the worship center)—people off the streets were invited to do meaningful work. Beier said that their mantra was, "If you want money, or if you want help, we will give you work to do." It became apparent that one of the best ways to serve their neighborhood was by giving people meaningful work. Seeing the promising results of this initiative, Beier then started a nonprofit economic development ministry called Hope Works.

Hope Works is focused on economic empowerment. It serves as an on-ramp for participation in the ministry, relationship-building, and discipleship. Striving to give people good, dignifying work has not been without its challenges. Many people off the street expect cash after working and not a paper check. However, they're seeing promising results. Beier recounted a story about a young man who has been with him for four years. The man did construction work for about six months before visiting the church and is now a member of the church. Another worker was dating a woman at the church but was also hustling and selling drugs. He was hired after visiting the church and continued coming. Eventually he was baptized and joined the church. On Father's Day of that same year, this man said, "I can't believe that I am celebrating Father's Day in a church with my family! I was hustling and selling drugs and you got me pounding nails and sweating and getting dirty and doing hard work. It's really difficult, but I'm enjoying it now."

Living Hope Church (and Hope Works) is establishing

a reputation on the Southside of Chicago. Once some college students were asked to canvas the neighborhood and hand out flyers. When they returned, Beier asked them how it went. They reported hearing comments like this from neighbors: "I got a job through Hope Works." Another guy said, "Oh yeah, that's my church, and they helped me with my employment."

Pastor Stan Archie, and Christian Fellowship Baptist Church, created an organization called the Community Impact Center. This center works with homeless male veterans and increasingly with women veterans. Partnering with Hope Faith Ministries of downtown Kansas City, they work with homeless people who struggle with drugs and alcohol addictions. Recently, Community Impact Center staff have identified and targeted neighborhood laundromats. There they pay for people's laundry and listen to their stories to assess how the church can serve them in concrete ways. With great excitement, Archie said, "Down the road they want to launch an urban version of Made to Flourish!"

Living Hope and Christian Fellowship Baptist Church reminds me of something that Pastor Reading, of United Evangelical Free Church (Seattle, Washington), said at the beginning of our interview. "Quit trying to be the best church in the city that competes with other churches. Be the best church for the city, so that if you were to shut your doors, the city would mourn." That's a good mandate for any church. Is your church competing or are you striving to be the best church for the city?

A Café : Prison-to-Work Training Ground

Joe Tucker is Executive Director of a nonprofit known as South Street Ministries. They run a community café called The Front Porch Café. This café is located one block from the Summit County Jail. Tucker said, "We're one block from a couple of other institutions that house inmates. And we're also in a neighborhood that was a local hub for a lot of recovery meetings."

Many of the workers at the café, in fact, come from backgrounds of incarceration, addiction, or poverty. Having workers with such backgrounds has been quite helpful; they're adept at distinguishing fact from the fiction. "Running such a ministry," Tucker says, "takes discernment." He explains, "So, a café staff member may say to a patron, 'Hey, man, this one is on us today. And since you're having a rough day, let's sit down and talk. Here's some eggs and toast.' However, if someone steps through our threshold and says, 'Hey, I'm looking for something to eat. I need something.' The conversation may go like this to discern if the person is a hustler or if the person genuinely needs assistance:

Café staff: "Sorry, we don't give money out loosely. If we don't know who you are, you could be hustling us. Would you help us clean the restroom for a bit today? And then we can get you a meal afterwards."

Patron: "No, I'm good today. I'll go somewhere else."

Café staff: "Okay, I guess you weren't that hungry after all."

Tucker said they have a lot of those interactions, and often they are preceded or followed by prayer. A lot of folks frequent the cafe enough that they know what's going on. "That's the ministry philosophy behind it," explains Tucker. "This practice separates the wheat from the chaff. It shows which folks are really ready to do the right thing versus the ones looking for a quick fix or quick money."

Sometimes Tucker and the staff will allow people to volunteer for a season for a variety of reasons. For example, the café has folks who volunteered to get a job reference. For someone like this, a café staff member might say, "Volunteer at the café for a few days. We'll give you meals, and you can take tips home. If you're a good worker, we'll write you a good reference."

Tucker added, "If we don't have a reference point for your workmanship, we won't recommend you to an employer. So often volunteering at the café is a test." Doing volunteer work is a great opportunity to see if the worker will show up on time and demonstrate integrity. It can all lead to gainful employment elsewhere.

The café's philosophy is working. The success has created a "good problem." They routinely lose their best employees because they move on to better jobs. Tucker and others were acutely aware of this problem because all of a sudden the food stopped being as good as it was before! The café, as a result, has had to tweak its philosophy and practice a bit to keep some of these "good stones." However, they still make room for people in need of work. "If someone crosses the café threshold and is just really trying to look for a job and discouraged" Tucker said, they still "help them out with that process." Still sometimes patrons just use the café as a public restroom or for the public phone or to use their tables and markers to write their cardboard signs. "Regardless, the cafe' staff will love on them," says Tucker.

Entrepreneurship: Walking with the Old and Young

Many churches are addressing the "E" in FWE by coming alongside and assisting those interested in being entrepreneurs. For instance, Mullins' past work includes an entrepreneurship initiative with the Uzbek refugee community. He connected entrepreneurs from his church with refugee entrepreneurs to help to start new businesses. The goal was for these startups to financially support the refugee entrepreneurs and their families. This effort was supplemented by providing English and citizenship classes.

Pastor Ward teaches entrepreneurship courses at Gordon-Conwell Theological Seminary in Boston, Massachusetts. From one class, 40 businesses were proposed and 30 of those 40 proposed businesses are still vibrant and running today! To help maintain that vibrancy, Ward and other mentors meet with these entrepreneurs every quarter.

At Abundant Life,[10] and in place of the traditional VBS, Ward's church sponsored a *BIZ Camp*. Here, young people, like his son, were taught how to develop business plans. Seasoned business leaders served as "sounding boards" to help these aspiring teenage entrepreneurs fine-tune their business plans and, eventually, launch new businesses. Ward's son's small business was so wildly successful that he put the local vending machines at his school out of business!

Tabernacle Community Church sponsored The Youth Entrepreneur Leadership Program. In this program, middle school students were exposed to entrepreneurship teaching for seven weeks during the summer.

Pastor Lindsay wanted to show these students that God has called us to be creators and to reflect His image as a creator.

During the summer, these students developed business plans and presented them to local entrepreneurs in a "Shark Tank" style environment.

Although missions and outreach is the least penetrated and developed area at Jefferson Assembly of God Church, Pastor Duncan is beginning to think about bringing small business development into some economically depressed neighborhoods. This is especially needed because people with limited resources, such as an unreliable vehicle, must drive 20 miles or more just to get to work. The church has also been looking at a program called "Strengthen Families" to help family units in these depressed areas. Duncan envisions using the principles in Steve Corbett and Brian Fikkert's book, *When Helping Hurts,* to foster far-reaching, long-term change.

Conclusion

Infusing FWE theology into the life of the church can be methodical and frustratingly slow, but rewarding. Pastors interviewed have spoken of their "awakening" to this important theology and are prayerfully seeking ways to integrate this theology into four areas in their local bodies: corporate worship, pastoral practice, discipleship/spiritual formation, and outreach and missions.

Some of their efforts have been met with success, while other efforts have not. Much of the progress, thus far, has come in the areas of corporate worship and pastoral practice. Most churches interviewed confessed that penetration of FWE theology in the areas of discipleship/spiritual formation and outreach have been slow. However, this is not because they don't deem these areas important; sometimes the reason for the slower progress is limited manpower, bandwidth, or knowledge on how to proceed. Nonetheless, we hope that this sampling of churches that are helping their congregants see discipleship as an all-of-life affair will inspire you. As you've met pastors and congregations that are helping their people connect Sunday to Monday, we hope it has sparked imaginative ideas that will help you implement a similar vision in your local church context.

Appendix A
Participants

Provided below are those quoted in this eBook. Feel free to contact them with additional questions.

Rev. Stan Archie
Christian Fellowship Baptist Church
Kansas City, MO

Rev. Ryan Beattie
Bellevue Presbyterian Church
Bellevue, WA

Rev. Brad Beier
Living Hope Church
Chicago, IL

Rev. Ken Duncan
Jefferson Assembly of God
Meriden, KS

Rev. Jason Harris
Central Presbyterian Church
New York, NY

Rev. Artie Lindsay
Tabernacle Community Church
Grand Rapids, MI

Rev. Jeremy Lile
City Hope Church
Akron, OH

Rev. Jim Mullins
(and intern, John Crawford)
Redemption Church
Tempe, AZ

Rev. Tom Nelson
Christ Community Church
Kansas City, MO

Rev. Mike Reading
United Evangelical Free Church
Seattle, WA

Rev. Jay Slocum
Jonah's Call
Pittsburgh, PA

Joe Tucker
South Street Ministries
Associated with Front Porch Fellowship Church, Pastor Crabbs
Akron, OH

Rev. Jon Tyson
Trinity Grace Church
New York, NY

Rev. Larry Ward
Abundant Life Church
Boston, MA

Appendix B
Most Cited Books

Dennis Bakke. *Joy at Work: A Revolutionary Approach to Fun on the Job.* Seattle, WA: PVG, 2005.

Craig G. Bartholomew and Michael W. Goheen. *The Drama of Scripture: Finding Our Place in the Biblical Story.* Grand Rapids, MI: Baker Academic, 2004.

Andy Crouch. *Culture Making: Recovering our Creative Calling.* Downers Grove, IL: IVP, 2008.

Steve Corbett and Brian Fikkert. *When Helping Hurts.* Chicago, IL: Moody Publishers, 2009.

Steve Garber. *Visions of Vocation: Common Grace for the Common Good.* Downers Grove, IL: IVP, 2014 .

I, Pencil. Article. http://www.econlib.org/library/Essays/rd-Pncl1.html.

Tim Keller and Kathryn Leary Alsdorf. *Every Good Endeavor: Connecting Your Work to God's Work.* New York: Dutton, 2012.

Tom Nelson. *Work Matters: Connecting Sunday Worship to Monday Work.* Wheaton, IL: Crossway, 2011.

Dorothy Sayers. "Why Work". In *Letters to a Diminished Church: Passionate Arguments for the Relevance of Christian Doctrine.* Nashville, TN: W Pub. Group, 2004.

Dorothy Sayers. "Creed or Chaos". In *Letters to a Diminished Church: Passionate Arguments for the Relevance of Christian Doctrine.* Nashville, TN: W Pub. Group, 2004.

Gene Veith. *God at Work: Your Christian Vocation in All of Life.* Wheaton, IL: Crossway, 2002.

Amy Sherman. *Kingdom Calling: Vocational Stewardship for the Common Good.* Downers Grove, IL: IVP, 2011.

Drew Cleveland and Greg Forster (Eds.). *Pastor's Guide to Fruitful Work & Economic Wisdom: Understanding What Your People Do All Day.* Waukesha, WI: Made to Flourish, 2014.

Os Guinness. *The Call: Finding and Fulfilling the Central Purpose of Your Life.* Nashville: Word Publishing, 1998.

Bruce Winter. *Seek the Welfare of the City: Christians as Benefactors and Citizens.* Grand Rapids, MI: Eerdmans,1994.

Christopher J. H. Wright. *The Mission of God: Unlocking the Bible's Grand Narrative.* Downers Grove, IL: IVP Academic, 2006.

Christopher J. H. Wright. *The Mission of God's People: A Biblical Theology of the Church's Mission.* Grand Rapids, MI: Zondervan, 2010.

N. T. Wright. *Surprised by Hope: Rethinking Heaven, the Resurrection, and the Mission of the Church.* New York: HarperOne, 2008.

About the Authors

SKYE JETHANI is an award-winning author, speaker, and ordained pastor. He served as both the managing and senior editor of *Leadership Journal* and as the director of mission advancement for *Christianity Today*. He currently co-hosts *The Phil Vischer Podcast*. Because of his diverse cultural upbringing and training in religious pluralism, Skye has been a sought after voice for groups facing challenges at the intersection of faith and culture, including The Lausanne Movement and The White House Office of Faith-Based and Neighborhood Partnerships. Skye has written for many publications including *Relevant* and *The Washington Post*, and he is a regular contributor to *The Huffington Post*. Skye is ordained with the Christian & Missionary Alliance and has served as a pastor in Wheaton, Illinois. He is a "Featured Preacher" on *PreachingToday.com*, and he speaks regularly at churches, conferences, and colleges in the U.S. and internationally including Q, Catalyst, Mars Hill Bible Church, and the U.S. Naval Academy. Skye has authored six books. His latest writing project is *With God Daily*, a subscription-based daily devotional that helps thousands in the smartphone generation begin their day with God.

DR. LUKE BOBO serves as director of resource and curriculum development for Made to Flourish, bringing leadership to creating and curating resources and curriculum for MTF pastors. Luke brings a rich blend of experience to MTF, having worked for 15 years as an electrical engineer before pursuing an M.Div. and Ph.D., and eventually serving as the executive director of the Francis Schaeffer Institute at Covenant Seminary. Luke has spent time as a professor of religious studies at Lindenwood University and currently works as an adjunct professor of contemporary culture and apologetics at Covenant Seminary. In addition to writing curriculum for a workplace ministry, Luke has written *Living Salty* and *Light Filled Lives in the Workplace*, and *A Layperson's Guide to Biblical Interpretation: A Means to Know the Personal God.* Luke has lectured and preached in Cape Town, South Africa and Goiania, Brazil. He currently serves as an elder at Paseo Baptist Church, Kansas City, MO.

MADE TO FLOURISH
A PASTORS' NETWORK FOR THE COMMON GOOD

Made in the USA
Columbia, SC
29 March 2019